101 THINGS
TO DO INSTEAD
OF PLAYING ON
YOUR PHONE

101 THINGS

TO DO INSTEAD
OF PLAYING ON
YOUR PHONE

ILKA HEINEMANN

Andrews McMeel
PUBLISHING®

Andrews McMeel Publishing
a division of Andrews McMeel Universal
1130 Walnut Street, Kansas City, Missouri 64106

www.andrewsmcmeel.com

17 18 19 20 21 RLP 10 9 8 7 6 5 4 3 2 1

ISBN: 978-1-4494-8529-0

Library of Congress Control Number: 2016957057

101 Things to Do Instead of Playing on Your Phone was first
published in German in 2014 by Verlagsgruppe Droemer Knaur
GmbH, and in English in the UK in 2015 by Short Books.

Editor: Patty Rice
Designer/Art Director: Holly Swayne
Production Editor: Erika Kuster
Production Manager: Tamara Haus

for Valentin

Introduction

If you're reading this book then you've noticed it too. Wherever you go, chances are that pretty much everyone you see is on their cell phone, checking their e-mails, playing Candy Crush, or updating their news feeds. It's a habit we are no longer even aware of.

Yes, smartphones are an incredible invention. But are we becoming so reliant on them that we are missing out on other things?

What if we started interacting with the world around us, or had a conversation without being continually interrupted? What if we could daydream again, or simply just relax?

Imagine a world where you are not constantly connected, where your mind is free to wander . . .

If you get stuck on any quiz questions or brain-teasers, find solutions at: shortbooks.co.uk/101-things-solutions-pages

1.

Reflect on something that made you happy in the last 24 hours.

2.

Look around you and try to find:

1. Someone wearing red pants

2. Someone with a mustache

3. A green car

4. Something spiky

5. Something round

3.

Play the animal game.

. . . where each new animal name
starts with the last letter of
the previous one

e.g., turtle, elephant, tiger . . . etc.

4.

Study the lines
on your palm.

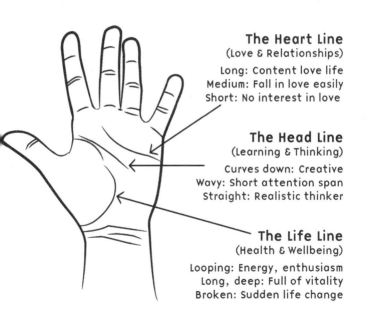

The Heart Line
(Love & Relationships)

Long: Content love life
Medium: Fall in love easily
Short: No interest in love

The Head Line
(Learning & Thinking)

Curves down: Creative
Wavy: Short attention span
Straight: Realistic thinker

The Life Line
(Health & Wellbeing)

Looping: Energy, enthusiasm
Long, deep: Full of vitality
Broken: Sudden life change

5.

Imagine that your life is turned into a movie.

1. What genre would it be?
   - [ ] a road movie
   - [ ] a romcom
   - [ ] a horror movie

2. Which actor would play you?

   _____

3. What would the title be?

   _____

6.

Perform this inconspicuous workout for the buttocks.

Stand straight with your shoulders
back and slightly bend at the knees.
Gently lift one leg at the knee.
Hold and count to twenty.
Return your foot to the floor.
Repeat with the other leg.

7.

Draw a selfie:

8.

Reorganize your purse or bag.

9.

Make a list of the ten best books you've ever read:

1. ....
2. ....
3. ....
4. ....
5. ....
6. ....
7. ....
8. ....
9. ....
10. ....

10.

Smile at someone;
see if they smile back.

11.

Play Boggle! How many words can you make from the letters in:

ANAESTHETIC

e.g. *ethics*

12.

Reflect upon a philosophical question.

Fate or free will . . . ?

What is truth . . . ?

Does time only flow one way . . . ?

13.

Color in this mandala.

It'll help clear your mind.

14.

Use the grid below to practice your multiplication tables:

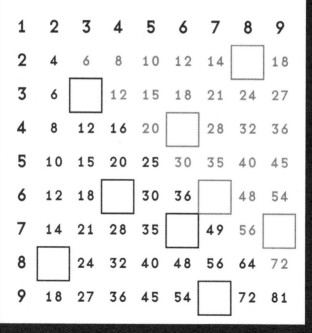

1	2	3	4	5	6	7	8	9
2	4	6	8	10	12	14	☐	18
3	6	☐	12	15	18	21	24	27
4	8	12	16	20	☐	28	32	36
5	10	15	20	25	30	35	40	45
6	12	18	☐	30	36	☐	48	54
7	14	21	28	35	☐	49	56	☐
8	☐	24	32	40	48	56	64	72
9	18	27	36	45	54	☐	72	81

15.

Can you match up these foreign idioms with their meanings opposite?

1. "Neither the horse nor the tiger."
   (Mandarin)

2. "Don't let go of the potato."
   (Canadian French)

3. "Have a goose to pluck."
   (Swedish)

4. "In the mouth of the wolf."
   (Italian)

5. "Don't hang noodles on my ears."
   (Russian)

Translation of foreign idioms:

a) "Good luck."

b) "Don't give up."

c) "Don't take me for a fool."

d) "Have a bone to pick."

e) "So-so."

16.

Limber up for your day by turning circles with your shoulders and then your ankles.

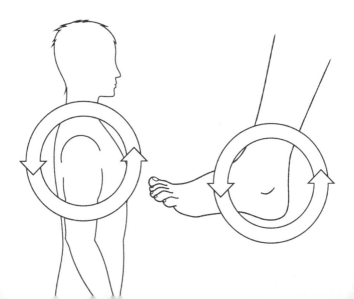

17.

PLAY FASHION ADVISER! HOW WOULD YOU IMPROVE THE OUTFITS OF THE PEOPLE AROUND YOU?

18.

Memorize as many of these things as you can.

You might be tested later.

1. knitting needle
2. stamp
3. football
4. cat
5. cell phone
6. ladder
7. balloon
8. watering can
9. key
10. fish
11. sunglasses
12. pear
13. screwdriver
14. leaf
15. socks

19.

simply concentrate on your breathing.

Breathe in deeply through your nose.
Hold for five seconds and exhale slowly.
Repeat.

20.

Make notes on how to get started on one project you've always wanted to tackle.

My Project:

21.

Draw a portrait of
the person you love
most of all.

22.

Write a cryptic crossword clue for this word:

5-Across:

....

....

....

e.g., An allied vessel forges camaraderie

23.

TRY

THESE

EYE EXE

RCISES:

1. Look to each corner of your vision: top-left, top-right, bottom-right, and bottom-left.

2. Hold your finger 8 inches away from your face. Focus on it as you bring it toward your nose.

24.

Imagine how a Martian would see the situation you are currently in.

How would you explain it to him?

25.

Do you know the reason why . . . ?

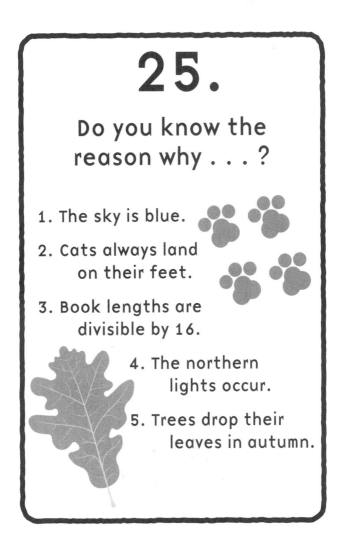

1. The sky is blue.

2. Cats always land on their feet.

3. Book lengths are divisible by 16.

4. The northern lights occur.

5. Trees drop their leaves in autumn.

26.

Reflect on
how you feel
at this moment
and
make the face
that fits
your mood.

27.

And the award goes to . . .

Which of your friends and family would win the award for being:

1. Most likely to make a million.

2. Most likely to get locked in a restroom.

3. Most likely to have a famous Internet cat.

4. Most likely to become a hermit.

5. Most likely to run a pyramid scheme.

28.

Were you concentrating?
Write down the items from
activity #18 without looking back:

1. ....
2. ....
3. ....
4. ....
5. ....
6. ....
7. ....
8. ....
9. ....
10. ....
11. ....
12. ....
13. ....
14. ....
15. ....

29.

Write a postcard to someone you haven't seen in a while.

30.

Riddle:

I have a mouth
but don't eat,

I have a bank
with no money,

I have a bed
but don't sleep . . .

What am I?

31.

Write a list of ten places you absolutely want to go to.

1. ....
2. ....
3. ....
4. ....
5. ....
6. ....
7. ....
8. ....
9. ....
10. ....

32.

Impress people today by using as many of these long words as you can:

1. Apricity — The warmth of the sun on a winter's day

2. Evanesce — To fade gradually from sight; vanish

3. Petrichor — The scent of rain on dust or dry earth

4. Lugubrious — Mournful or gloomy to a ludicrous degree

33.

"Those who cannot change their minds cannot change anything."
— George Bernard Shaw

Identify three limiting beliefs you hold and change them for productive ones.

Example:
Limiting belief:

I find it hard to speak my mind

Productive belief:

My opinion matters

Limiting belief:

Productive belief:

Limiting belief:

Productive belief:

Limiting belief:

Productive belief:

34.

Add the European capital cities.

35.

Clear

your mind.

Don't think.

Just be.

36.

Write down what you thought about when your mind was meant to be clear.

37.

Complete checkmate
in one move on the
board opposite.

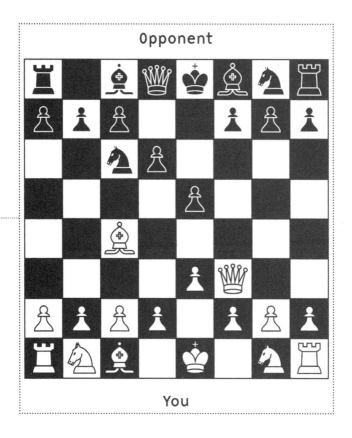

38.
Pick a flower or
a leaf and dry
it in this book.

39.

Can you wiggle your little toe?

(When did you last check
it was there?)

40.

Now **discover** how your body is **feeling** by moving your focus up from your **little toe** all the way to the **top of your head**.

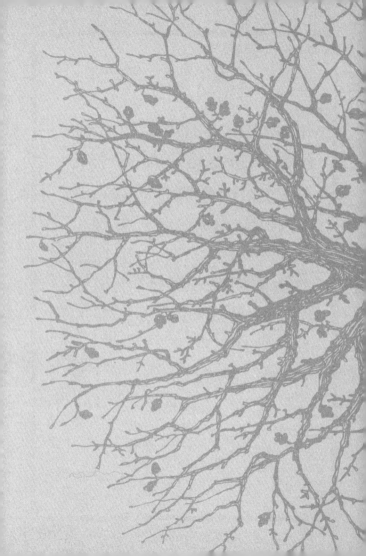

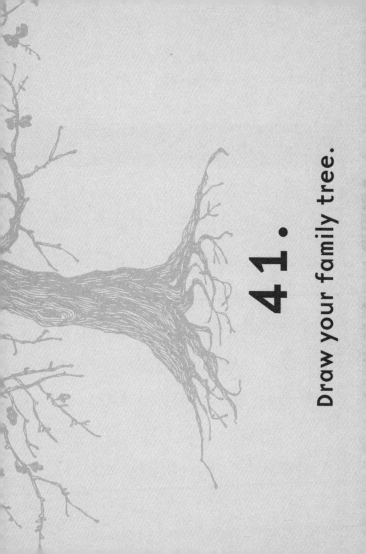

41.

Draw your family tree.

42.

"I dont know whos chosen the music or whose album is playing, but its got lots of songs from the 1960s and Johns really into Sixties music, so perhaps its one of Johns CDs."

43.

Write an advertising slogan for:

1. Your favorite hobby

2. Your favorite drink

44.

Cut out the page opposite and make a paper airplane.

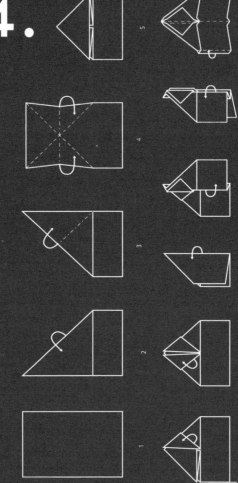

45.

Try to recall the
telephone numbers
of your three closest friends.

Name:
☎

Name:
☎

Name:
☎

46.

Think of your
very first
childhood memory.

47.

Picture the thing that is bothering you.
Mentally turn the image to gray and
blur the resolution.
Imagine it getting smaller
and smaller until it is only a
dot in the distance.

48.

Think of an image that represents what
you want to achieve.
In your mind, increase the contrast
and brighten the colors.
Now magnify the image
so that it fills your vision.

49.

Plan how you would
redesign your living room.

50.

Write a poem that includes the following words:

sex, asphalt, traffic lights, Easter bunny, tomato, gray.

....

....

....

....

....

....

....

....

....

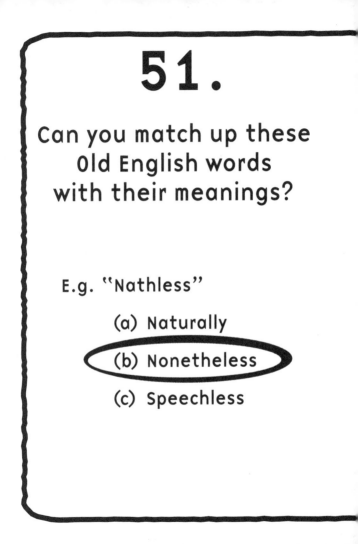

1. "Floytinge"

    (a) Showing off

    (b) Singing

    (c) Whistling

2. "Bawdrik"

    (a) Belt

    (b) Trousers

    (c) Indecent

3. "Sikerly"

    (a) Unwell

    (b) Certainly

    (c) Unlikely

Answers: 1c, 2a, 3b

52.

Look at the people around you—who would you like to have coffee with?

ZZz

53.

Power nap!

Statistics show that just 20 minutes of napping in your day can reduce your risk of burnout.

54.

"The quick brown fox jumps over the lazy dog."

Devise another sentence that uses all the letters in the English alphabet.

Letter checklist:
A - B - C - D - E - F - G - H - I - J - K - L - M
N - O - P - Q - R - S - T - U - V - W - X - Y - Z

55.

Doodle here:

56.

Decide what you will prepare for dinner tonight.

57. Write your grocery list for the meal:

58.

Circle which of these values best describes you:

courage

wisdom

balance

honor

kindness

loyalty

reliability

sensitivity

modesty

open-mindedness

59.

Use the next page
to write a friendly or
surprising note to
a stranger . . .

Cut the page out of the book
and place it somewhere where it
can be found easily—and
hopefully make someone's day.

Important message!

60.

What animal would you like to be reincarnated as?

61.

....

....

....

....

....

....

....

....

....

The art of getting things done?
Write your bucket list!

62.

Think of how these names sound when read backward:

1. The name of someone you love.

2. The name of your boss.

3. The name of your old math teacher.

4. The name of your favorite sports personality.

63.

Write down your favorite joke

....

....

....

....

. . . or, if you can't think of one, memorize this:

Yesterday, a clown held the door open for me.
I thought it was a nice jester.

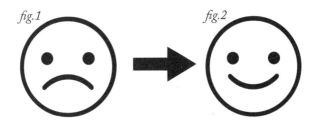

fig.1   *fig.2*

64.

Think about where
you will be in ten
years' time.

65.

Improve your marketing skills.

1. Write a pitch for your current job.

....

....

....

....

....

....

2. Describe your current location in Realtor speak.

....

           .

....

....

....

....

....

3. Write a tourist guide to your hometown.

....

....

....

....

....

....

....

תראה, איזה ספר
הבחור הזה קורא?

אין לי מושג –
משהו על
טלפונים חכמים.

66.

Listen to a conversation
in a language you do
not understand and
try to imagine what it
might be about.

67.

The 7 chakras of the Hindu tradition are all about striking a balance in your centers of energy. Mark your position on each of these scales:

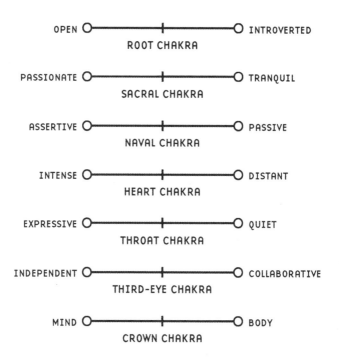

OPEN O————|————O INTROVERTED
ROOT CHAKRA

PASSIONATE O————|————O TRANQUIL
SACRAL CHAKRA

ASSERTIVE O————|————O PASSIVE
NAVAL CHAKRA

INTENSE O————|————O DISTANT
HEART CHAKRA

EXPRESSIVE O————|————O QUIET
THROAT CHAKRA

INDEPENDENT O————|————O COLLABORATIVE
THIRD-EYE CHAKRA

MIND O————|————O BODY
CROWN CHAKRA

68.

Remember five things you did last week.

Monday
_____
_____
_____
_____

Tuesday
_____
_____
_____

Wednesday
_____
_____

Thursday
_____
_____
_____

Friday
_____
_____

Saturday
_____

Sunday
_____

69.

Cloud zoo!
Look up at
the sky
and find
the animals.

70.

Practice this simple meditation technique

1. Concentrate on your breathing, the rise and fall of your chest.

2. Pick a word or a phrase to keep in the forefront of your mind.

3. Whenever your thoughts drift, bring them back to the phrase.

4. Let your emotions flow by and simply watch them as they pass.

71.

Complete this
dot-to-dot

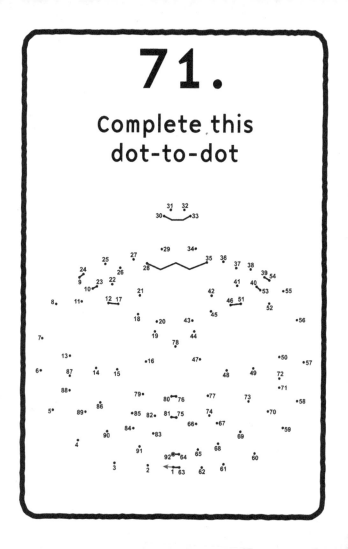

72.

He wishes for the Cloths of Heaven

Had I the heavens' embroidered cloths,

Enwrought with golden and silver light,

The blue and the dim and the dark cloths

Of night and light and the half light,

I would spread the cloths under your feet:

But I, being poor, have only my dreams;

I have spread my dreams under your feet;

Tread softly because you tread on my dreams.

—*William Butler Yeats*

73.

If you had to give up any of the below for a month, how would you cope?

chocolate   coffee

shopping   television

Facebook   headphones

arguing   lying

74. Draw a comic strip.

75.

Write a loving letter to someone you care for.

76.

Close your eyes and
travel in your mind to
a Caribbean island . . .

What sounds can you hear?

77.

Write down a short list
of names you wish
you had been called.

1.

2.

3.

4.

5.

Could having a different name
have changed your life?

78.

Make a resolution
to pay someone a
compliment today.

79.

Can you recognize these leaves?

Clockwise from top left: ash, oak, beech, sycamore

80.

. . . And how about these birds?

Sleek black plumage; yellow beak and yellow around eye

Scruffy feathers; brown, black & gray with black patch on throat

Brown back & wings; gray, speckled breast

Navy back & wings, red throat, and pale breast; tail streamers

Clockwise from top left: blackbird, sparrow, swallow, thrush

81.

Look at the people around you and imagine the lives they may be leading.

82.

Pick someone to offer your seat to (without causing offense!).

83.

Write down the poem from activity #72 without turning back the page.

He wishes for the Cloths of Heaven

—*William Butler Yeats*

84.

Devise your own mnemonic for remembering the names of the planets in the solar system.

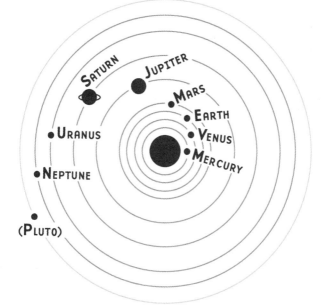

e.g., My Very Easy Method Just Speeds Up Naming Planets

85.

"We are what we repeatedly do."
— Will Durant

45% of what we do every day is performed without a moment's thought.

Make one small change and you may find it leading to something big.

For example:

Put your running shoes by the front door.

Take a different route to work.

Cross your arms the opposite way.

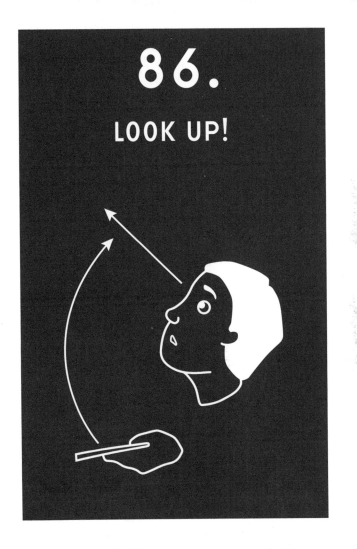

87.

Write your own
bedtime story

so you are not stuck
for ideas when
you next need one.

Once upon a time . . .

....

....

....

....

....

....

....

....

....

....

....

88.

Spare a moment to think about the first person you kissed.

89.

Complete this sudoku:

	8			9	3	2	6	
	2		4	1				
		9					4	
			7		4	9		3
2	7					4		5
		4		8	5			
9	5				7			2
				3	1			
3		2			8		7	4

90.

Try this relaxation technique.

Rub the palms of your hands together until they become warm and put your hands over your eyes.

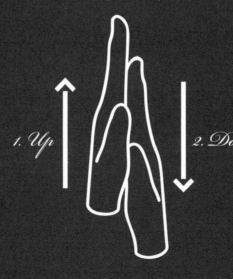

1. Up   2. Down

91.

Think of three things you would take to a desert island.

1.
....

2.
....

3.
....

92.

Count the number of
smartphones you can
see people using . . .

Count the number of people
reading **books** . . .

Which one wins?

VS.

93.

Try to remember all the lyrics from your favorite pop song.

94.

Try and figure out
which of your **five senses**
is the strongest.

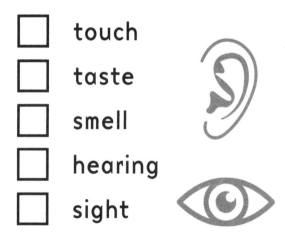

☐ touch

☐ taste

☐ smell

☐ hearing

☐ sight

95.

Work out these anagrams:

SPAREDMAN

BIGHERON

96.

Imagine what the
people around you
look like naked.

If you haven't done so already.

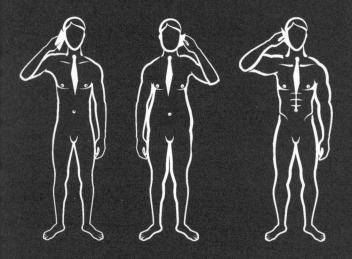

97.

Sharpen your mind
by solving these math
problems in your head:

564 + 213 = ...

896 − 239 = ...

13 × 16 = ...

168 ÷ 28 = ...

98.

Make a list of your ten favorite songs:

1. ....
2. ....
3. ....
4. ....
5. ....
6. ....
7. ....
8. ....
9. ....
10. ....

99.

Focus on the bigger picture.

We often get bogged down in the stress of every day.

Thinking back on your life so far, what has been really meaningful? And which of your current preoccupations will simply dissolve away?

100.

Now you've found out
all the things you
could be doing
instead of playing on
your phone . . .

Write a break-up
note to your cell
phone.

It's not me, it's you . . .

101.

CARPE
DIEM
Seize the day!